EMOTIONAL INTELLIGENCE 2.0

Achieving Success Through
Emotional Intelligence
(2023 Guide for Beginners)

Clara Lucas

Contents

Introduction

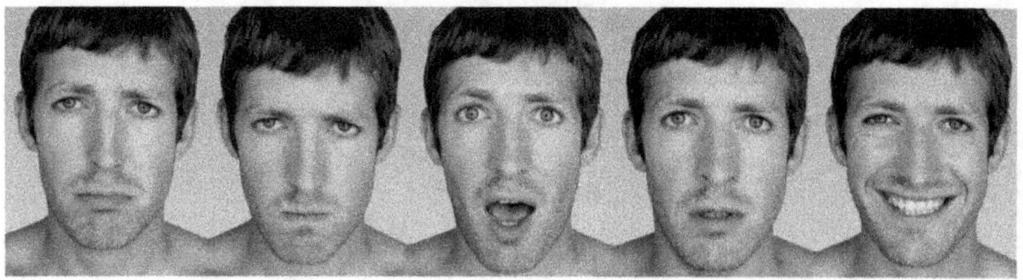

Emotional intelligence is the collection of skills involved in self-awareness. Emotions, as well as controlling one's emotional reactions to both positive and negative events. Emotional intelligence is made up of self-awareness, self-image, self-control, empathy, impulse control, and a lack of impulse. Recently, the general public has begun to understand the significance of emotional intelligence.

Social awareness, intuition, and the capacity to control emotions are all components of emotional intelligence. Emotional intelligence is the ability to "read" the emotions of others around you as well as your own. This enables individuals to convey their reasonable thoughts and ideas successfully. Moreover, emotional intelligence may either help or hinder personal progress; it can be seen as a positive factor that promotes personal development and growth through embracing oneself for who one is at any given moment. Yet, a lack of emotional intelligence might stifle development. This is because when things are going well, one may feel hopeless and try to alter anything in their lives to "fix" an issue they did not have in the first place. In some ways, a person is imprisoned by their own views. Mirror neurons in the brain enable you to feel the emotions of others, giving you a better grasp of the world around you. Feeling connected to a person or situation helps a person grow by making them more aware of and present in their own lives. This leads to personal growth. People with more emotional intelligence are more resilient when they face problems, which helps them grow and learn from their experiences.

Emotional intelligence means knowing how you feel and being able to figure out how other people are feeling. This suggests that emotional intelligence includes not just what you can think or feel but also how you perceive how others feel or think. Here, "feeling" rather than "thinking" enters the picture. Emotional intelligence is a mix of social awareness, insight, and the ability to deal with feelings in different situations. People with high emotional intelligence may be able to understand and connect with others better, which can help them get along and be understood. They may also be able to control and manage their own emotions in certain ways.

Emotional intelligence is the next big thing in psychology. It is thought to be the most important set of skills to improve relationships, health, happiness, and success in your career. Research has shown that emotional intelligence is linked to success in every area of life. As the field of positive psychology has grown, it has become clear that we need to improve our emotional intelligence skills if we want to be happier. Emotional intelligence is especially important for preventing violence and school shootings, which are big problems in our society right now.

Emotional intelligence can also help you deal with everyday problems like improving your relationship with your partner or children. Since it improves your capacity to manage relationships and decreases stress, emotional intelligence may help you live a happier, more successful life.

For numerous years, scientists have been studying Emotional Intelligence; it has been connected to various issues, including stress management, emotions, relationships, health, and success. In 1997, Goleman wrote the Harvard Business Review essay "Emotional Intelligence." In it, he talked about how emotional intelligence was the key to success. Goleman's award-winning book, Emotional Intelligence: Why It May Matter More Than IQ, was released in 2006. Since then, the amount of research on how emotional intelligence affects people has grown a lot and become more organized. Research has shown that emotional intelligence is key to success because it helps people understand and control their emotions. Emotional intelligence influences how we handle stress and may improve the quality of our lives. Successful individuals surpass others on standardized IQ tests but not on emotional intelligence exams.

CHAPTER 1

Why Do We Need Emotions?

Some scientists think that emotions are the outcome of evolution, while others feel that they are essential to human existence. And while it's impossible to know for sure if one theory is right, we do know that emotional reactions keep us safe from dangerous situations and help us make quick decisions.

Fear, for example, may make it simpler for you to flee from someone who grabs you on the street. Your body sends warning signs even if you don't consciously believe he is dangerous. This is why we have these innate responses to some things.

Some experts feel that emotions are responsible for our ability to communicate with others. A grin, for example, communicates to others around you that you are content. It may seem straightforward, but our facial expressions and emotions interact in complex ways. These encounters enable us to express ourselves without saying anything.

The chemical release is a major component of emotions. When something frightening occurs, your heart rate increases, and your breathing rate increases. These changes happen because your body makes chemicals like adrenaline and cortisol that get your body ready for physical activity. Even though it may not seem like a huge concern at first, it is a crucial aspect of controlling your body and mind.

Although it may seem that emotions and the hormones that govern them are harmful to our health, we need them to live. We would be able to operate in the world even if we did not have emotions. These substances assist us in getting things done. They help us get up when we're tired and go to sleep when we're too tired to do anything else. These substances also assist us in feeling better once these events occur.

This is why we have these innate responses to some things. Although emotions are not always beneficial to our health, they should not be avoided. We need them to exist and operate properly in the world.

The Core Emotions

The core emotions are a set of seven emotions that are regarded as the main or basic emotions. Disgust, wrath, fear, sorrow, pleasure, intrigue, and surprise are among the fundamental emotions. Some studies have found new emotions that are part of the core emotion group, such as disgust and laughter.

Several studies have also found that other emotions are similar but not in this basic group. Even though these emotions aren't part of the core emotion group, we still think of them as emotional states that greatly impact how we understand our own emotions. Shame, remorse, pride, and success are some of these emotions.

Even though there is a lot of debate about whether or not these other feelings should be on the list of main emotions, one thing is for sure. We all go through the main emotions regularly, whether we recognize them or not. Even if we can't explain or define our feelings, that doesn't mean we aren't feeling them on some level.

Theories of Emotion

A variety of ideas have been presented to explain why people feel emotions. Some of these theories are about how emotions have changed over time, while others are more about how emotions affect our thinking. There is no one right answer, but most scientists think that the interactions between the different theories help us understand human emotions better.

Evolutionary Theory

An evolutionary explanation is one hypothesis of emotion. According to this view, emotions emerged in humans through the process of reproduction. It was thought that emotions were created to assist humans in finding someone with whom they might make a link. This would help these people protect their children and ensure that their DNA, passed down through their children, is passed on to future generations.

This idea explains why emotions seem to cycle. In a logical progression, certain emotions seem to lead immediately to others. For example, we feel happy and optimistic when we feel attracted to someone. We often experience sensations of love and affection when these feelings are returned. Strong feelings of attachment are made so that the relationship is more likely to last in the future. This makes us want to find deeper connections with this person.

Cognitive Theory

The second way of thinking about emotions is that they come from how our brains process information. People think that our limbic system is activated when we see or hear something that makes us angry. This part of the brain stem is called the "emotional center," and it is responsible for making feelings from experiences that we don't say out loud.

When our limbic system is stimulated by something, it makes us feel pleasure and happiness. This is because our brain reacts to precise impulses and produces awe. People think that these pleasant feelings are "rewards" that help us learn new things because they make us feel good.

This theory makes sense regarding how emotions are communicated, but it does not explain why feelings exist in the first place. So, it's thought that the way the brain processes information plays a role in how we feel. Although there is no need for a more sophisticated theory to describe this, it may still be best explained by including both ideas.

Type of Emotions

Emotions are often categorized as either basic or complicated. A fundamental emotion is one that can be communicated just via facial expressions. Even when they are mild, these emotions are usually very straightforward to identify. Joy, sorrow, wrath, fear, and contempt are examples of basic emotions.

Complex emotions are those that cannot be represented just via facial expressions. They may be hard to recognize in some situations because they don't have facial expressions or other behaviors that make them easy to spot. Pride, love, and guilt are examples of complex emotions.

Gender Differences

Some emotions are experienced differently by men and women. People have noticed that shame is more common in women while guilt is more common in men. This may be because men and women are socialized differently. Research conducted in the United States discovered that, although women experienced emotion on a deeper level than males, men had more violent sentiments than women.

We all encounter emotions on a daily basis. We may not always identify our emotions, but that doesn't imply they don't exist. Emotions may be communicated from one person to another, allowing individuals experiencing the same emotion to recognize others experiencing the same emotion.

It may be evident that we have emotions, yet there are some that we do not identify as such until we examine our own. That does not imply that you should let your emotions dictate your life, but it may be beneficial to be aware of what is happening inside you to understand better how to cope with everyday events.

Why Are Some People More Emotional Than Others?

To some degree, everyone feels emotions. Having said that, some persons are classified as emotional. You may believe you are more emotional than others because you cry at a sad story or laugh loudly at a comedy.

There is no obvious explanation for why some individuals feel emotions more intensely than others, although it might be related to how our neurological system is built. Some people are born with a lower emotional threshold, while others are better able to hold on to memories that are strong enough to make them feel stronger emotions.

In any case, you may learn to manage your emotions more efficiently. This could make your feelings less strong and help you avoid situations that make you feel too much.

Your Emotional Response Toolbox

The tools listed below will assist you in dealing with emotions more effectively.

See emotions as belonging to you but being outside of your body. This will help you separate yourself from the feeling and look at it without getting caught up in it.

Consider yourself to be outside of your body, peering at a silent movie playing in front of you. This will help you perceive emotions as something external rather than personal.

If you are emotionally reacting to anything, stop and think about what occurred before getting too worked up over it. Individuals sometimes respond emotionally without thinking about what triggered their sentiments.

Surround yourself with optimistic individuals. This can help you avoid circumstances that may cause you to get too emotional.

If you're feeling emotional, try to distract yourself with something else before doing anything you'll regret later or that will elicit even more emotion.

Use relaxation methods before going to bed and if you are feeling emotional. This can help you relax and deal with circumstances that elicit strong emotions.

Work out on a regular basis. Endorphins are chemicals that make you feel good and give you a sense of euphoria when you exercise.

Emotions are reactions to experiences that make us all feel something. This can be a good thing, but it can also be bad when emotions take over and make people do things they later regret.

CHAPTER 2

The Personal Competencies of Emotional Intelligence

Components of Emotional Intelligence: Self-Awareness

How well do you understand yourself? Can you articulate who you are while recognizing your internal and external experiences? Are you aware of your own personal resources? Why is it so tough to explain oneself in interviews or on dating websites?

In its most basic form, self-consciousness is an awareness of oneself. The self-comprises several components, such as your talents, ideas, and experiences. Self-awareness as a notion has existed since the time of ancient civilization when a Greek philosopher summed it up as "knowing yourself." Lao Tzu, a Chinese philosopher, took a more in-depth look at self-awareness. "Understanding others is intellect, knowing oneself is genuine knowledge, dominating others is strength, and mastering yourself is true power," he said.

Although these ancient thinkers had a good idea about self-awareness, it wasn't until 1972 that the first research was done on the topic. Shelly Duval and Robert Wicklund, two psychologists, conducted this investigation. Duval and Wicklund's research sought to determine if a person could pay attention to themselves or their surroundings at any given time. According to the findings of this study, a person may concentrate inwardly or outwardly, depending on the circumstances. For example, you might be deep in contemplation or actively aware of what is happening around you at any time. Duval and Wicklund went on to write a book on objective self-awareness that is still relevant today.

In their work, Duval and Wicklund said that self-awareness is a key part of self-control. They emphasized that you can only govern your conduct to meet your standards and beliefs if you are aware of it in the first place. In other words, if you pay attention to your emotions, you'll be in a better position to comprehend why you feel them in the first place. At the same time, if you pay attention to your habits, you are more likely to know how to control them as well.

For instance, let's say you have a coworker who always gets on your nerves. You have yet to comprehend why this is the case since you never take the time to consider why you are constantly adversely affected by their presence. But now that you've read this book and understand how self-awareness works, you decide to spend some time thinking about yourself. You notice that this coworker is often complaining about other people's weight. You also understand that you are sensitive about this subject since your weight, although no longer a concern for you today, was a continual issue for you as a child. You now understand why every conversation you have with such a coworker seems like an assault on you. You are also better positioned to control your actions and conduct toward your coworker.

For example, you may opt to avoid this individual, or you could attempt to explain to them why discussing other people's weight is disrespectful. Obviously, the coworker will need to learn about self-awareness to know which topics are okay to talk about and which ones are not. Oddly, this coworker is completely unconscious of their acts and influence on others, and as long as they are, they will continue to insult others. Their lack of awareness arises from their lack of knowledge of their own self and how they interact with themselves and their surroundings.

How well do you know yourself? These are some questions you may answer to determine your level of self-awareness:

1. Have you ever seen yourself in the mirror while doing anything like eating?

2. How do you feel when someone you know well criticizes you? Are you angry, disappointed, or more intrigued about why they feel this way about you?

3. Do you consider yourself a jealous partner? If you said yes, do you feel jealous all the time, or do you think your jealousy is fair?

4. Are you the sort of person who loves to have someone to blame when something goes wrong or do you simply go with the flow and put it up to bad luck or other unexpected circumstances?

5. Have you ever felt the desire to or really thrown a tantrum when engaging in sports or any other competitive activity?

6. Do you think you're empathetic to others? Have you ever been accused of being too sympathetic?

7. Can you read other people's emotions?

8. How often do you vent your frustrations on someone else?

9. Do you consider yourself to be particularly sensitive?

10. Do you stay strong with your political and religious ideas or allow for flexibility?

These are just a few questions you could ask yourself to figure out how self-aware you are as a whole. If you answer the questions sincerely, you will undoubtedly see a trend by the sixth question. People who don't know themselves well are more likely to look for reasons for their actions outside of themselves. They often cannot control their emotions and prefer to blame someone else. The signals that separate a person who is not self-aware from the rest of the crowd are obvious to everybody.

Characteristics of People Who Are Not Self-aware They Are Bullies.

As part of a campaign to stop bullying in schools, kids have been repeatedly told that bullying is a form of being a coward. Bullies are, indeed, cowards. Bullies do not go away; instead, they grow up, which is a cruel truth that people face many years after they leave the playground. Adult bullies exist, and they share the same places as we do. They go to the same churches as us, work in the same areas, and have similar musical tastes.

A bully's conduct arises from the fact that they are afraid of something, but instead of facing the cause of their fear, they choose to terrify someone else. Bullies show how little they know about themselves by putting their energy in the wrong place. If you frequently bully others, you may lack self-awareness and need to dig within yourself to figure out what you are afraid of.

They Are Highly Controlling.

To be honest, the majority of us like to have control over many parts of our life. In fact, you should never let your life spiral out of control if you can avoid it. Regrettably, for many people who are not self-aware, the drive for control is all-consuming and reaches even into the lives of others.

Why is this the case? As humans, we often battle with many aspects of our life that may not always go as planned. When someone who isn't self-aware faces something they can't handle, they try to make up for it by trying to control other things. A person who is failing at their career, for example, may attempt to rule their house with an iron hand. If these individuals were self-aware, they would recognize the source of their desire for control and make reasonable efforts to refocus their attention.

They Prefer to Be Passive Aggressive.

Regardless matter how outgoing a person is, there will come a moment when an awkward discussion is unavoidable. We are human beings with diverse genetic origins and sociocultural settings, and we are going to conflict in some fashion at some point. When this occurs, the prudent thing to do is to sit down and speak things out so that the occurrence does not happen again.

However, those who are not self-aware do not view it this way. They don't like being put in situations where they have to face problems straight on. Therefore, they resort to passive aggression as a problem-solving strategy. Since they are terrified of addressing what is concealed deep inside themselves, these people may keep the mask on and seethe on the inside by becoming passive-aggressive. Being passive-aggressive is frequently emotionally taxing and never addresses the matter at hand. It makes one side feel used and mistreated, and it leaves a lot of room for misunderstanding.

They Have a Whole Lot of Made-Up Reasons That Do Not Involve Being Accountable.

When you have a serious lack of self-awareness, you will never be able to recognize the events in your life for which you are accountable. Instead, you will go through life seeking to blame someone else. If you are late for work, you will blame traffic rather than the reality that you got up thirty minutes late because you stayed up late the night before. People who are continuously looking for an excuse to hide their tracks have yet to master the art of reflection. Sure, life happens, and things go wrong from time to time. But, as people, we are occasionally to blame for what happens. It doesn't harm to hold oneself responsible in this situation. In reality, this demonstrates maturity and self-awareness and will gain the respect of others around you.

They Suffer from Delusions of Grandeur.

Some individuals feel they are so talented in their craft, only to fail spectacularly when it comes time to present it to an audience and/or a judge. You may have seen them on major talent programs like American Idol and Britain's Got Talent. You've undoubtedly evaluated them from the safety of your sofa, wondering how they thought they could sing/dance/put on a magic show when they clearly don't have any skill. You may have even wondered why their friends or relatives never warned them that they are hopelessly bad at singing/dancing.

The fact is that if a person is not self-aware, you cannot rescue them from their own illusions of grandeur. Even though it has been shown that people with mental illness are more likely to have delusions of grandeur, other people can also have them. Thinking you are more spectacular than you are is a terrific boost to your self-esteem and something we could all use from time to time. But, there is a reasonable limit beyond which you move from self-assurance to utter fantasy. Self-awareness aids in the suppression of this misconception. Self-awareness balances out your self-image so that, although you know you're beautiful, you're also aware that you're not the gorgeous person in the world.

CHAPTER 3

Ways to Improve Your Self-Awareness

The nice thing about self-awareness is that you can practice it and develop it regardless of your current level of self-awareness. You may go from being completely unaware to the most self-aware you've been in years. You can completely change how you see yourself, both inside and out, by using tried-and-true methods that you can use in your daily life.

Observe Yourself

The first step is to become an observer of yourself and your life. Nonetheless, you must maintain your objectivity and neutrality as an observer. When doing this observation, you cannot evaluate yourself. If you are judgmental, you will miss vital information and take notes along the way. It would help if you guaranteed that you are simply taking notes on what is going on in your life—the emotions you are experiencing and the thoughts you are having throughout the day—while resisting the need to add a comment here and there.

For example, suppose you just ran into your workplace crush in the office kitchen. You exchange pleasantries, and then, because you're anxious, you ramble on about something that didn't need to be stated. Take notice of the current situation and your sentiments. It's easy to dismiss this as a dumb and cringe-worthy experience you don't want to relive. Nevertheless, doing so will simply leave you vulnerable to repeating the same incident, which is precisely what you are attempting to prevent. Regardless matter how uncomfortable a scenario is, you should make a note of it and return to it later to have a thorough grasp of it.

If you are unsure if you recall everything that occurred to you throughout the day, maintain a notebook. A diary is useful because you can always go to it when you need to reflect on how you are feeling, even if it has been many days.

Set Aside Time for Introspection

After taking sufficient mental notes, it is time to begin the analyzing process. This is most likely to happen towards the end of the day, right before you go to bed. This is the finest time since you have finished dealing with the world for the day and can be honest with yourself in the privacy of your own house. The soul-searching that will occur at the end of the day will provide you with the chance to discover why you behaved the way you did throughout the day.

Why did you yell at your coworker immediately before lunch? What made you so angry? Why did you contact your ex, whom you said you'd never call again? Why did phoning him make you feel so lonely and unimportant? Everything that occurs under the sun has a legitimate explanation and a fundamental cause. You are well on your way to being more self-aware if you can pinpoint the core cause of all your thoughts and emotions. And do you know what you can make out of roots? You may uproot them if they are not the kind you wish to feed.

Ask Your Friends and Colleagues to Tell You What They Really Think About You

When it comes to learning how others see us, trusted friends may be really beneficial. Request that your close friends describe you in the most honest and non-harmful manner possible. This informal feedback will provide you with insights into how you seem and interact with people.

You may have always thought of yourself as a pleasant person, only to discover that your pals see you as a bully. Do not take offense if this occurs. Instead, look at this as a chance to grow as a person whenever you can, and ask your friends to help you figure out when you act like a bully. So, you'll know when you're being a bully without even realizing it.

Shift Your Mindset

You best believe it when they say it's all in your head. We discussed emotions and the function of the brain in their creation in the introduction. You may assist yourself in feeling emotions that are good and useful to your human experience if you can rewire your brain.

For example, experts claim that whenever you suppress your rage and choose a more tranquil choice, such as walking away, you are teaching your brain to help you become calmer. That is something you can simply test at home. What is the one thing that truly irritates you? Is your internet connection slow? When your internet provider reduces your speed, resist the urge to lash out and hurl objects at your computer. Instead, get up and take a short stroll about the neighborhood. Experiment with this a few times. You will no longer feel the need to be furious over sluggish internet connections after the third time. In any event, what's the worst that might happen if you lose your internet connection for a few minutes? Yeah, the globe will send numerous gigabytes of data without your help, but things might be worse, right?

Aligning your emotions and ideas with your value system is also part of shifting your thinking. We often do things simply because that is what has always been expected of us. Knowing what you value as a person will result in a much-needed paradigm change, which will be a signifi-cant step toward self-awareness.

Forgive Yourself

We are wonderful at providing grace and forgiveness to others when they are in need, but we aren't so good at doing it for ourselves. You will learn that some of your views or things you have adhered to as indisputable facts were not. This might come after periods of contempla-tion and interactions with others.

When you reach this stage, you must release all judgment and hatred against yourself and unconditionally forgive yourself. This implies you must also forgive yourself for any dumb ideas, acts, or sentiments you may have throughout the course of your day. Remember how uneasy you were in the presence of your workplace crush? It would help if you also forgive yourself for this. It is a necessary component of the learning process.

Start Anew

You can start over as a self-aware person if you have a new understanding of your emotions and ideas and a critical look at the value system that shapes them. Self-awareness is not a one-time event. Often, you will forget and return to the old and familiar. That's the problem with humans: We want to go back to what we know because it feels safe. As tempting as it may be to return to your comfort zone, keep in mind that change is frequently difficult and uncomfortable. Being self-aware may seem difficult, but it is precisely what you need to become who you are intended to be while building meaningful and respectful connections with others around you. You may have to face some personal demons along the road, but the end result will be well worth the effort.

Practice Meditation and Mindfulness

Many individuals go about their daily lives while awake and on autopilot. Few people get to experience the awareness that comes from connecting with their deepest selves. You will need to practice meditation and conscious awareness to do this.

Mindful awareness is a word used to describe the increased consciousness that comes from being in touch with your thoughts, emotions, feelings, and experiences at all times throughout your waking life. Mindfulness is precisely how you will be able to take note of your experiences throughout the day, giving you information to chew about afterward.

Mindfulness also gives you power over your life. It is the distinction between passing through life and enjoying life. In one, you are a pawn pushed about by your emotions, while in the other, you are the queen directing the shots.

Several meditation applications are available on both the Google Play Store and the Apple App Store to assist you in learning how to be more attentive as you go about your day. One way to stay alert and calm is always to be aware of your breathing and try to figure out how you feel on the inside before letting it show on the outside.

CHAPTER 4

Components of Emotional Intelligence: Self-Regulation

Those who are self-regulated or who have emotional intelligence (EI) can keep their emotions under control. Most of the time, they can keep their cool in tough situations and don't act rashly out of anger or irritation. These successful people may not always make the best decisions, but they do show their feelings when it's appropriate to do so.

The capacity to govern your emotional reactions is referred to as "self-regulation." It's the difference between acting like a kid and acting maturely like an adult. To some degree, everyone can self-regulate, but it is a talent that may be honed with time.

To learn to control your emotions, you often need to take a step back and look at the bigger picture. You can see the bigger picture by giving yourself a moment to think before you act. When you're in a situation that makes you feel bad, it's important to ask yourself what you can learn from it. Self-control is a skill that takes time and works to develop, but everyone can get better at it.

The capacity to recognize your own emotions is an important part of emotional intelligence. When you can perceive your own emotions, you may better comprehend why they happen. Identifying your own emotions is a useful first step toward self-regulation. Think about your emotions and how they make you feel in your body. This information will assist you in identifying them in the future. Don't simply ponder about your emotions; pay attention to how they make you physically feel.

Steps To Improve Self-Regulation

1. Establish Your Own Values. Values are basic views about the world. They may be emotionally charged, and they influence your daily activities. Establishing personal values is an excellent strategy to improve self-regulation. Values are the things in the world that you care about the most. Knowing your own beliefs allows you to lay the groundwork

for your life and select what steps to take to effect good change. You can also use them to help you set goals, make decisions, and spot opportunities. It's frequently beneficial to speak with a trusted friend about what's important to them and how they see the world.

2. Accept accountability for your actions. Accept responsibility for your actions when you make a mistake. Nobody is flawless, and no one has complete control over everything that occurs to them. Difficulties are unavoidable, but there is only one thing you can do when they occur: learn from your errors and move on because no matter what happens in life, no matter how tough the situation may be, there is always another opportunity to set things right. Understanding you can't control everything will make you feel more at ease about taking risks and attempting new things.

3. Make calm and collected your default state. Your mood will alter how you see the world. Individuals with good self-regulation are frequently calm and composed. Make tranquility your objective if you want to be more emotionally savvy. When you see yourself becoming agitated or upset in a situation, remember that it is just a sensation.

You may alter your mood just by changing your thinking about it. When you are worried or upset, take deep breaths because getting more oxygen into your body will help calm you down.

4. Practice breathing: At moments of stress or height-ened emotions, be aware of your own breathing patterns. Be aware of how your breathing varies when you are anxious or unhappy, and strive to regulate your breathing in order to control your mood.

5. Balance sentiments vs. logic: evaluate the advan-tages and disadvantages of reacting to a high-stakes situation with emotion and logic. Does it require passion and emotion, such as deciding to propose to someone?

6. Make your objectives clear to people around you: Making your goals public holds you responsible for them. What better way to motivate yourself in the team than to ensure that your objective is understood by others, particularly if it is a goal that directly impacts them?

7. Take a minute to count to ten before responding: When you are thrilled about something, take a few seconds to take a deep breath and mentally

count to ten. This permits the exhilaration to fade and prevents you from reacting to unpleasant emotions.

8. Give yourself a night off before making important decisions: It's natural to want to react emotionally when faced with a major decision. Instead of making such decisions purely on emotion, give yourself a night to think about it and let the more intense sensations dissipate.

9. Consult with self-management experts: Get advice from those around you who can regulate their own emotions. These folks may be able to provide you with guidance and ways to deal with their emotions.

10. Make an attempt to smile more: Our bodies often respond with emotion to physical stimuli, and smiling might boost your emotional perspective. Make an effort to smile and notice how your emotions begin to shift toward the good.

11. Make time every day for analytics: Make time to deal with the day's difficulties diplomatically. If you do this if an issue arises throughout the day, you know there will be time to fix it later if it can wait, and it becomes less stressful.

12. Manage your inner monologue: It's difficult to be outwardly optimistic and in control of your negative emotions when they run wild in your head. Keep your thoughts under control and away from negativity. Use recognized self-awareness practices such as meditation to keep your thoughts on track.

13. To remain motivated, drown out negative ideas with good ones: Set a goal of having two positive thoughts for every bad one. This silences negative thoughts and helps you perceive benefits you would not have considered otherwise.

14. Envision success for yourself: Develop a mental image of what you want to achieve. This way, you'll grasp what success looks like and be able to identify your objective.

15. Plan and carry out the steps required to achieve success: Begin planning the steps you will need to take to achieve your objective. If you want to be a more dependable friend, think about how you will be dependable and what steps you will need to take to make that happen, such as constantly following through on your promises.

16. Take care of yourself: Make sure you care for yourself. Take the time to exercise, eat sensibly, and pamper yourself to reduce stress.

17. Concentrate on your strengths and talents rather than what you can't do: If you concentrate on the bad, your whole attitude will be negative. Instead of concentrating on what you can avoid doing in a certain scenario, concentrate on what you can accomplish.

18. Make an effort to learn something beneficial from every interaction: There is something valuable to learn from every encounter, whether it's how your body movement or tone influenced another person or how you behaved in a certain circumstance. Make a point of finding something meaningful in interactions, particularly if you believe the experience was worthless.

19. Schedule a time to relax: If you want to concentrate on regulating your emotions, you need to maintain your stress at a manageable level.

20. Understand that you can improve these talents and that your existing limits are not permanent: Your self-control is neither basic nor restored.

Remind yourself that you have the ability to influence others, for better or worse.

21. Be prepared to control your negative sentiments when they arise: If you have a difficult time responding properly in specific situations, attempt to devise contingency plans that will assist you in reducing undesirable behaviors or notions. If the tension becomes too great, you will have something to fall back on.

22. Strive to encourage patience while discouraging the pleasure principle: You want to avoid being impulsive or making choices only on emotion. After you have been patient and sensible in the face of a circumstance, try to reward yourself.

23. Employ body language to control your emotions: If you maintain a calm posture in your body, your mind is more likely to follow through than if you actively prepare for a struggle.

CHAPTER 5

Components of Emotional Intelligence: Motivation

Suppose you have a really tight deadline at work and are under a lot of pressure to complete the assignment on time. Maybe a large deal is dependent on your activities in the coming hours. Maybe your career is at stake. What would your reaction be? Most of us would be quite concerned, especially if our livelihood were at stake. As a consequence of your anxiousness, you are more likely to put in additional hours, begin the assignment early, and even seek assistance from colleagues. You reacted emotionally and felt anxious, so you did something to finish the task and make yourself feel better. On the plus side, your feelings for your partner may put you under pressure to propose marriage. You could also look for activities and situations that make you feel good, like being happy or excited and avoid those that make you feel bad, like being sad or bored.

If our emotions are the engine that drives us, and self-control and self-regulation serve as the steering wheel and brakes, then this is about the gas pedal. You may go all Spock and suppress your emotions, but that's like yanking the accelerator off your automobile. Never leaving the driveway may be safer, but you will never go anywhere. A high EI indicates that we not only understand what drives us but that we can also manipulate our emotions to get us where we want to go.

Those with a high EI live by design, motivated by a sense of purpose and meaning, which provides them with internal motivation. These individuals are more prepared to react to problems because they have a long-term vision of where they are headed and why they are getting there.

We gravitate toward our default patterns when we live without design. We will become trapped in a rut with our job, income, health, time, speech, and relationships if we are not purposeful, and ruts will never lead us somewhere new.

Indeed, some individuals are more driven by themselves than others. Nevertheless, like many other things, motivation can be built up and developed. We'll look at three approaches to boost your motivation: reasons, routines, and relationships.

Reasons: Find Your Passions

"Choose a profession you like doing, and you will never have to work a day in your life," famously stated Mark Twain. The quote is fantastic. It inspires us to discover the meaning behind what we do. That is to say, and passion is an important component of motivation. Humans are enthusiastic about numerous topics, and although everyone's interests vary, they are what motivate us.

So, what are your interests? Could you provide any examples? What role do they play in your daily life? Identifying your hobbies is essential for finding inspiration, even in your daily activities. They might be the fuel that keeps you going day after day.

Does this imply that you should only do things that thrill you? Not precisely; often, our passion isn't directly related to what we do but to why we do it—or for whom we do it. Some folks, for example, are not very enthusiastic about cleaning dishes—quite the contrary. Nonetheless, they will still get up early to accomplish things since they know their spouse or family would appreciate it. So their passion isn't cleaning the dishes but rather loving their spouses, families, or whoever they're doing it for. Doing something we don't love is sometimes the finest approach to discovering what we are enthusiastic about.

Understanding our passion stems from a healthy sense of self-awareness. Not only should you be aware of your present emotions, but you should also be aware of what you enjoy and dislike. And it would be best if you were deliberate about utilizing them to motivate yourself. Identifying our particular interests and incorporating them into our daily and weekly schedules will provide us with the energy and inspiration we need when we need it the most.

Pursuing our interests is a more motivating motive than the biggest compensation (unless the highest salary allows for another passion). It will not only make us happier but also enable us to accomplish a better job. Identify your interests, label them, and include them in your weekly calendar. That will have a significant influence on your motivation. It's also vital to recognize that interests might change over time. Experimenting with different hobbies might help you uncover new interests and sources of inspiration.

Routine & Novelty: Every Few, Do Something New

We need both regularity and novelty in our lives to enhance our drive. When things seem out of control, the routine structure may help us retain a feeling of order. The novelty of new activities, on the other hand, contributes to our inspiration.

Whatever else is going on in the world, there is one thing that everyone will do (nearly) every day: make their bed. This regimen gets their day started. Repetition produces outcomes.

Simultaneously, performing the same activity again and over might lead to boredom. We need novelty in addition to routines. The introduction of new activities inspires us by providing us with energy. We don't work seven days a week because of this. We need to take pauses and do something new to reenergize ourselves.

Individuals who regularly exercise must include new routines into their regimen. It kept them engaged by concentrating on distinct body objectives.

We will quickly become weary of doing the same old thing if we do not include fresh experiences in our fitness program. As a result, it isn't easy to remain motivated. In short, we will exhaust ourselves. Still, trying a new workout or activity can give us new energy, which can give us new ideas for our life, career, and relationships.

"For every few, do something new," says one useful rule. Introduce something fresh every few regular encounters to revitalize and motivate you.

Some individuals are inherently inclined to regularity, while others are naturally drawn to novelty. Repetition and creativity are inextricably linked.

A good combination of habit and novelty may help you develop a rhythm that will assist you in getting into the groove. A healthy rhythm that combines habit and novelty will keep you motivated and enhance your job and overall well-being.

Relationships: Competition, Accountability, and Encouragement

Relationships are another significant aspect of our drive. Even if we conduct the majority of our job alone, our interactions with people will inspire us. This occurs largely via three types of relationships: competitive, accountable, and encouraging.

We are usually aware of people who arrive earlier or remain later than us at work. We push ourselves to follow suit and put in the time necessary to flourish in our jobs. Watching people go above and beyond inspires us to do the same. When individuals compare their own performance to that of someone who began at the same time, it creates a healthy incentive. This drive motivates people to challenge not just one another but also themselves. Competition can be a great source of motivation as long as it doesn't get out of hand.

Accountability ties are another form of drive.

For example, a group of guys gets together twice a month to catch up, share life experiences, and barbeque. They also agree to read and discuss a book together. This has become such an essential source of inspiration in their life that no one wants to show up to the monthly gathering and be the one who hasn't completed the reading. The person would feel like he'd let the other men down and wouldn't have as much fun as if he didn't keep up. These accountability connections enable them to do more than they could on their own.

Recall that accountability connections push us harder than we can push ourselves.

Similarly, if we want to commit to regular exercise but find it difficult to get out of bed for our morning run or show up at the gym at the end of a hard workday, we may benefit from joining a running club or finding a workout partner. Knowing that someone with running shoes would be waiting for us on the corner of the street encourages us to stop creating excuses and get the workout we need and desire. Having someone keep you responsible for reading, exercising, or actively boosting your emotional intelligence will be a terrific motivator.

Finally, encouraging interactions help us stay motivated when we are weary, sad, or ready to quit.

While going through the expected hard patches, encouraging relationships becomes crucial. For instance, consider a relationship that you believed would work out but did not. It takes time to recover from such losses, and in the absence of that connection, we need to hear from others who know and care about us. When people check in with a phone call or a text message and provide encouraging words, we are strengthened in ways we could not accomplish on our own.

Another hiccup may be a job loss. Spending day after day looking for new jobs is difficult, particularly when we learn that the positions have been filled by someone else, but we must persevere. This is exhausting, which is why we need people to sign in. It's uplifting when folks not only inquire how we're doing but also remind us of our previous accomplishments and positive attributes.

Without it, we may feel tempted to give up. Nevertheless, suppose we have individuals who support and encourage us. In that case, we are more likely to keep going—sending out great applications, being confident in ourselves when we interview, and being ready to contribute when the proper time arises.

We all get a lot of motivation from the competition, being responsible, and supportive relationships. Yet, if we know ourselves well, we will realize that some are more useful than others.

Remember, when we know ourselves, we know what drives us; use that information to your advantage.

So, how about you? What connections have the biggest influence on your motivation? What motivates you the most: healthy competition, accountability, or encouragement? Is it because one of these is missing that you're feeling unmotivated? Utilizing these categories will assist you in identifying and using your most effective sources of inspiration.

Applying Your EI

What life interests would you wish to pursue further in your life? Make a list of one or two that seem unexplored. What practical ways can you provide an opportunity to explore those? Please take note of how investigating them promotes drive in other aspects of life.

What comes easier to you: habit or novelty? Which of these is the most difficult? Consider where you want to improve—perhaps by adopting a weekly fitness plan. Maybe it's incorporating new things into your regular routine, such as going for a walk to celebrate the end of the week or volunteering in your neighborhood. In any case, resolve to do "something new every few" in the next week. Take note of how this mix of habit and surprise will motivate and invigorate you.

Staying motivated requires relationships of competitiveness, accountability, and support. Which of the three forms of relationships works best for you? Which of the following is presently missing in your life? Do you know someone that exemplifies that kind of relationship? Please make time to talk with them about building deeper ties in this area in the coming months.

Fire Social Competencies of Emotional Intelligence

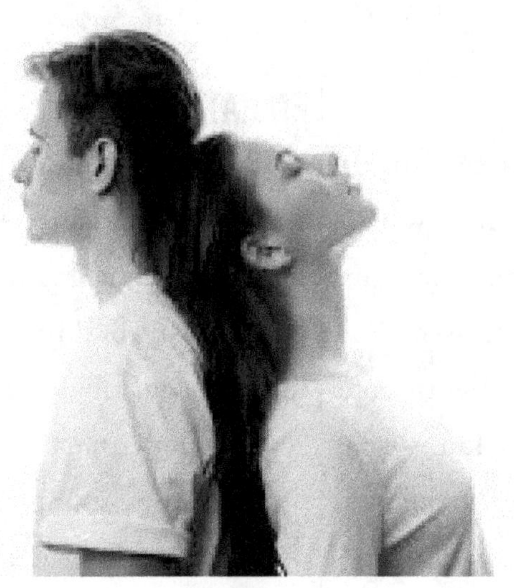

Components of Emotional Intelligence: Empathy

Empathy, not compassion, is what you experience when you put yourself in another person's shoes. In comparison, compassion is essentially sadness dressed up. You sense a person's sorrow and ideas when sympathetic to them. If they are in a crisis, it is as if you are in a crisis yourself. Empathy is a more devoted form of compassion, which may explain why many individuals don't have time for it. Empathy requires time and patience. It is not as simple as holding a pity party for someone and then moving on. Empathy requires you to stay and hunt for a solution to that person's pain since their suffering is also your suffering. People often confuse empathy with pity. According to our previous definition, this is both wrong and deceptive. Let's examine some instances of compassion and empathy.

SYMPATHY	EMPATHY
You encounter a buddy attempting to reduce weight for quite some time. She seems exhausted and stressed. You have never battled with your weight, but you know that losing weight may be difficult, and you inform her of this.	Your buddy then meets another acquaintance who has tried and succeeded in losing weight. This buddy expresses to your acquaintance that they actually understand and know what they are going through since they have gone through the same thing. Since they have gone through a similar situation, the second buddy can relate to and connect with your friend's issues.

Cancer has been diagnosed in your friend's mother. Your buddy is heartbroken. She is particularly close to her mother being an only child. Over the course of a year, you'll see her try to balance employment and being the only caretaker for her mother. You can't help but feel tremendous pity for both of them as your friend's mother's life ebbs away.	Your other closest buddy has suffered the heartbreak of losing a parent to cancer. They completely understand what your buddy is going through right now. They understand the anxiety of not knowing how to go without their major cheer-leader. They have seen first-hand the anguish of witnessing someone you care about disin-tegrate under the weight of a fatal disease.
Your employer, a well-known businessman, makes a terrible investment and loses all of his money. Because of this unex-pected development, he must declare bankruptcy. When you hear this news, you say to yourself, "Wow, being in such a circumstance must be quite tough." Although you realize that losing all of your money must be difficult, you have not experienced it yourself and can only sympathize.	Your boss's pals have made poor business judgments in the past. Some have even reached the edge of bankruptcy and almost lost their families as a result. They understand and can relate to the intense emo-tions that come with losing all of your money and assets. Therefore, they are sympathetic to your boss's dilemma.

In actual life, compassion and empathy differ from one another, as seen in the table above. It is crucial to emphasize that you do not have to have been in a person's precise situation to be sympathetic. Alternatively, you may teach yourself to see things from other people's points of view in order to become more sympathetic. For example, you don't have to have lost a pet to understand and sympathize with a pet owner who has. If this were the case, only a select few who had experienced hardship and life-altering experiences would be capable of empathy. Empathy, on the other hand, is something you can practice and improve at.

Empathy is a difficult talent to master; therefore, it goes without saying that it must be practiced diligently. Many individuals who assume they are empathic are really merely sympathetic. The good news is that you can improve your ability to put yourself in other people's shoes. When it comes to developing stronger interpersonal interactions, a person who has mastered empathy is well ahead of the competition.

Types of Empathy

Although empathy is described as the ability to connect with and empathize with another person's pain, it encompasses much more than that. There are three distinct sorts of empathy; thus, it is essentially three things. The area of the brain responsible for empathy is where the difference is found. Cognitive empathy, social empathy, and empathetic concern are the three forms of empathy.

Cognitive Empathy

Cognitive is an adjective derived from the word cognition, which refers to the act of gathering information and then processing it via the mind and the rest of your senses. Cognition is sometimes known as perception, reasoning, or insight. This description of cognition makes it simpler to understand what cognitive empathy entails.

Cognitive empathy is the discipline of viewing things through the eyes of another. Cognitive empathy requires us to look at information as if we were viewing it through someone else's eyes rather than merely processing it from our own viewpoint.

Many things influence our views. Some of these characteristics are inherited, while others are the product of our upbringing and the settings in which we find ourselves. A few common influences on perspective include age, ethnicity, gender, nationality, experiences, needs, and even innate skills. Since these elements may generate billions of permutations, every one of the world's seven billion people has a highly distinct viewpoint on things. Cognitive empathy requires us to strive to see the world through the eyes of the individuals we engage with rather than imposing our own views and judgments on them.

Cognitive empathy is not necessarily a natural trait for most individuals.

Most of the time, individuals are obstinate in their beliefs and hesitant to consider other viewpoints. Others will quickly go into Mr. Fix-It mode, failing to see that the other side just wants to be understood.

Emotional Empathy

Sharing another person's emotions is known as emotional empathy. Emotional empathy is also known as affective or primal empathy. For example, you will almost certainly cry if you see a sad movie. You didn't make yourself weep; it simply occurred. There is a scientific reason for why people weep watching movies and how this relates to empathy.

Your body is more likely to produce oxytocin at extremely moving parts in a film. Oxytocin is a hormone that is frequently referred to as the love hormone since it causes us to care for others. While you are under its influence, you become more empathic and are therefore more inclined to weep during a tragic movie scene, even if you know it is all made up. Of course, research into the relationship between oxytocin and empathy is still in its early phases, and we won't know for sure what's going on until these studies are finished.

Empathetic Concern

It is a sort of empathy in which you feel the sorrow and suffering of other people and attempt to alleviate it. The sympathetic concern is the ability to notice another person's pain while also stepping in with a solution that will assist them to be free of the anguish. It is also known as compassionate empathy, shown by millions of individuals who aid during times of crisis, such as earthquakes, hurricanes, tornadoes, etc.

The finest kind of empathy is frequently sympathetic concern since it entails not just demonstrating sympathy for another person's pain but also intervening to ensure that they do not have to suffer any longer. Those who need empathy the most don't always want to be understood or weep alongside them. Instead, they desire someone to assist them in getting out of their predicament, and here is where sympathetic care comes in. If you are in a leadership position, it will be your best option for improving working relationships with your subordinates or team.

Yet, it is vital to remember that the various forms of empathy do not arise at different phases of your life. If you are the sort of person who is naturally sympathetic, you will often feel all three levels of empathy at the same time. While feeling many sorts of empathy at the same time, it is critical to be aware of which is most useful at the time.

For example, a doctor will not benefit from exhibiting excessive emotional empathy. Consider this: your surgeon in tears is the last thing you want to see as you're being carried into the operating room. Yeah, it's comforting to know that your surgeon understands your agony, but you really need their compassionate care while attempting to heal whatever is wrong with you.

Additional traits of an empathic person exist, but these are the most frequent. If you can connect to them, you are empathic, which is really beneficial and effective in any scenario. But if you aren't, there are certain things you may do to become more assertive. To begin, in order to become an empath, you must be able to see beyond yourself. Attempt to learn more about individuals and the environment around you. Not only should you discover new things, but you should also enjoy them. Selfish individuals are constantly blind to the bigger picture of their surroundings.

CHAPTER 7

How to Develop Empathy in Your Everyday Life

1. Begin by attempting to view things from the perspectives of others: This will help you understand that the people around you are not wicked, unreasonable, or obstinate but rather respond to events depending on the information that they have.

For example, don't constantly speak about yourself while on a date. Pay attention to the other individual as well. In this manner, you'll allow your date to tell you about themselves and their lives. Then you'll be able to actually get to know each other and pique the other person's curiosity.

2. Affirm others' points of view: By doing so, you will acknowledge that others have the right to believe differently than you since they have a different point of view.

For example, you believe that burgers are the finest meal at a certain restaurant, but your buddy disagrees. He believes the soup is superior. Try to figure out why he feels that way, and then sample the soup for yourself. Maybe you'll reconsider.

3. Evaluate your attitude: Don't always believe you're correct. If you want to become compassionate, have an open mind and an open attitude since you are not always correct.

For example, you may believe that your Computer cannot be repaired and that the best answer to your issue is to get a new one. Others in this position may have a different answer. Attempt to negotiate with them. You're not always correct.

4. Pay attention: Don't live in your own world. Listen to people using your ears, your eyes, and your heart. Only then can you become closer to others around you and comprehend how they think, feel, and experience things.

For example, if you're at a restaurant with a buddy and he's trying to explain why he didn't enjoy it there, pay attention to what he has to say. Put yourself in his shoes and attempt to understand why he feels the way he does.

5. the essential thing is to consider what others would do in your situation.

For example, always let people clarify their perspective if you are unsure about anything. If your employer is upset with you for whatever reason but not with the rest of the group, ask him why. If you are unhappy with the response and believe your employer is incorrect, put yourself in his position and attempt to view the problem through his eyes.

Begin by being more communicative and practicing all of these abilities. As a result, you will become an empathetic person, and people will have a good view of you since you will seem more accessible and kind in their eyes. Also, your interests will grow by listening to what others experience, feel, and think. It's a fantastic talent that will enable you to experience the world through the eyes of others.

This is the most important aspect of improving your talents. When you put yourself in the shoes of others and strive to comprehend their thoughts and experiences, they will share your interests and will try to picture and understand your world as well. In this manner, you will undoubtedly begin to create an environment full of pleasant individuals, cooperation, collaboration, and teamwork.

Ideas and suggestions for more empathic conversion and communication:

- Constantly pay attention to what is happening around you emotionally and physically.

- Pay close attention to what others are saying. Please take note of and memorize their keywords and stages.

- React positively.

- Be adaptable; alter course when others' sentiments and opinions shift.

CHAPTER 8

Components of Emotional Intelligence: Social Skills

In the context of emotional intelligence, social competence is a wide phrase that refers to the abilities required to manage and affect other people's emotions effectively. Although this may seem to be manipulation, the fact is that it is as easy as realizing that giving people your smile makes them smile as well. Your grin has the power to make someone feel a lot better and more cheerful than they were before.

Consider social skills to be the last element in the emotional intelligence jigsaw. Only when you understand and control yourself will you be able to comprehend and influence other people's emotions and sentiments.

Some of the most important social skills are as follows:

Persuasion Skills

Persuasion is the skill of persuading or influencing someone to do something they would not have done if they had not interfered. (Persuasion is not to be confused with its more sinister cousin, manipulation.) Whether you are in a leadership position or not, you must understand how to persuade others to do what you want them to do. Before you can influence somebody, you must first read them properly in order to understand what appeals to them. Persuasion is a talent that salespeople have utilized all over the globe to persuade clients that they need to purchase a certain product.

Communication Skills

This aspect of emotional intelligence is crucial. It would help if you listened to what people were saying and effectively communicated your ideas and emotions.

You may be wondering what qualities a good communicator has. You are an excellent communicator if you can listen effectively to others, grasp what they say, and seek open and complete information exchange. You are an excellent communicator if you are willing to hear others' concerns as well as their good news.

Dealing with difficult issues, putting things straight, and not permitting bothersome difficulties are what good communication entails. To guarantee that the message is correct, you must ensure that you record and respond to emotional cues while speaking.

Leadership Skills

This may seem unusual, but keep in mind that leadership qualities are all part of social skills. Leadership is greatly influenced by emotional intelligence, not the other way around. It is important to emphasize that emotional intelligence and leadership abilities are intimately related. As previously said, only those who are tuned into their own emotions as well as the emotions of others around them, have a chance of influencing others.

Influence and the capacity to draw people along with you are important characteristics of excellent leadership. You might call this charisma, but the fact is that leadership is much more than that. It's superior emotional intelligence, in a nutshell.

A successful leader must be able to express a vision and inspire people with it. It makes no difference whether you are formal or informal; the key is to ensure that you provide leadership, support, and guidance to the individuals you work with, hold each person responsible and lead by example.

Conflict-Management Skills

We are all aware that disagreements may happen at any moment. They seem to emerge out of nowhere. Nonetheless, resolving disagreements as they occur is essential at home and in business. It all starts with developing our understanding of the value of diplomacy and tact in dealing with problems in diverse scenarios.

To be a competent conflict manager, you must be ready to bring issues to the surface when resolving them. It would help if you guaranteed that you utilize information sharing to foster debates and open conversations, reduce hidden currents, and assist each side in understanding the other's sentiments and logical stance in order to reach a win-win solution.

Understanding Emotional Drain and Energy Vampire

Signs of Emotional Drain

We are all aware that life is not easy. There are so many ups and downs, mountains and valleys, highs and lows to deal with, and you never know what to anticipate. There are moments when life is too difficult for us to manage anything. It doesn't matter what the cause is, but the reality is that life always finds a way to knock us down.

We fail to see that we become emotionally and cognitively exhausted when we suffer. The difficulty is that the consequences of these are visible. Our vitality is depleted to the point that we are physically drained, and all we can do is break down. It would help to recognize when life is too much for you to regulate and manage your emotions properly. These are some warning indicators to check for:

Insomnia

Do you have difficulties falling asleep? This might be connected to your emotions. When you are emotionally exhausted, you are more likely to have insomnia. You may believe that you will fall asleep quickly since you are agitated. Yet, insomnia happens often because you spend the majority of your time in deep contemplation, battling with the demons in your brain, and having difficulty obtaining a decent night's sleep.

Lack of Motivation

When you're emotionally depleted, you don't seem to care about doing anything. You no longer have objectives that get you out of bed in the morning. You're simply riding the tides of life and letting them carry you wherever they want. You begin to disregard your career, health, cleanliness, and family.

Hopelessness

This indicates that you are emotionally exhausted. After you've pushed, struggled, and clawed your way through the storms, all your energy is depleted, and you start to wonder why you're bothering when things don't seem to get better. This is the point of no return, and it is very hazardous. When you reach this stage, you risk lifelong agony and suffering because you have accepted that this is your way of life. If you've reached this stage, it's time to get assistance.

Detachment

If you've been hit hard by life, it's easy to isolate yourself from the people around you. You have allowed suffering to become a part of your life to the point where you are numb to it because you have been through so much that reality no longer exists for you.

It would be best if you determine what is draining your emotional reserves. Is it your spouse, family, friends, coworkers, or boss? What do you do when someone drains your reserves of energy?

- You are always thinking about them.

- You're fatigued physically.

- When they depart, you discover happiness.

- They do not help you.

- You feel the urge for some break after being together for a while.

- They expect too much from you.

- When they speak, they leave you feeling even more irritated than before.

- You can't seem to articulate what you mean when you're among them.

Constant Crying

Crying is something that most individuals abandoned throughout their adolescence. We become better at managing and controlling our emotions as we get older, and we only weep when something significant occurs in our life. Others, on the other hand, have been pushed to their breaking point, and sobbing has fast become a way of life for them - a sad movie makes them cry, someone wrongs them, and they cry, or an old friend requests forgiveness from them, and they cry.

When you weep readily like this, it indicates that you are emotionally weary. In other words, even the tiniest emotional trigger causes you to cry.

Irritability

When you are emotionally exhausted, you have emptied all of your emotional and mental reserves to the point that you have no tolerance for anybody. You may find yourself becoming irritable to little irritations. Someone next to you may be chewing noisily, and you'll be battling the impulse to strike them in the face. Earlier, you could dismiss this obvious lack of table etiquette without giving it a second thought. There is an obvious link between stress and rage, and it is easy to see even without the assistance of a psychologist. Consider this: When you feel yourself snapping most at those around you—perhaps your husband or perhaps your children? When you are anxious, chances are you are less enjoyable to be around.

CHAPTER 10

How to Deal with Energy Vampires

As previously said, energy vampires are all around us. Depending on your circumstances, you may also be an energy vampire. For example, depending on what you are going through, you may be exceedingly needy and codependent at periods in your life. If you've ever required someone to fill an empty space or meet a need in your life, you were undoubtedly an energy vampire at the time.

Is there any use in learning how to cope with the fact that we all have the potential to be energy vampires? Wouldn't it be simpler to merely remain in our natural forms as well-intentioned but rather needy individuals who occasionally drain the soul out of others without meaning to? Unfortunately, there are vampires that will leave a trail of emotionally depleted humans in their wake without feeling any guilt. An energy vampire of that kind may wreak havoc, which is why it is critical to understand how to cope with the purposeful and calculated emotional vampire.

When dealing with an energy vampire, you must first identify them for what they are. We often engage with the wrong individuals for a long time before we realize what they are and the harm they bring to our lives. Consider this a red sign that you want if the emotion you experience after spending time with someone is consistently bad. As humans, we have a tendency to lavish grace and forgiveness on individuals who do not deserve either.

We suggest they were possibly having a poor day or are coping with difficult circumstances in their lives. We make excuses for folks when we know deep down that they are terrible for us and are not having a bad day. If someone consistently acts like a jerk, they are most likely a jerk. Let such a person continue getting away with it just because you are polite to them.

While dealing with energy vampires, it is critical that you learn how to center yourself. Knowing who you are, understanding yourself, and keeping true to yourself are all part of grounding yourself so that you are not easily persuaded by individuals who come and go in your life.

It would help if you had a clear and strong awareness of your own personality and energy. Energy vampires have a method of spotting susceptible individuals who they may exploit. Those who are readily persuaded are considered vulnerable. For example, if you are easily shaken by what others think and say about you, you will be ideal prey for emotional vampires.

Consider yourself to be a strong oak with roots that go deep into the soil. This oak stands firm in rain or shine. Be an oak. Let the energy vampires exhaust themselves while thinking about how to uproot you.

Always remember to keep your personal space safe. Personal space serves as a barrier between ourselves and the outside world. Preserving your personal space entails being selective about who you let into your life. You will set yourself up for a lot of grief and emotional depletion if you make it simple for an energy vampire to enter into your personal zone.

Although it is wonderful to be pleasant to everyone you meet, it is not your responsibility to be friends with everyone. It would help if you thoroughly screened everybody who comes into contact with your personal space.

Imagine sitting across from an energy vampire for an hour as they drain your soul. Isn't it draining? But, if you sit next to this vampire in a group, their bad energy is distributed among the three or four of you. If you really must interact with an energy vampire, think about doing it in a group environment to safeguard part of your energy.

If your boss, for example, is an energy vampire, resist the temptation of a one-on-one working lunch. Instead, go for group meals that include the whole staff. Of course, this is sometimes beyond your control since your employer may want to put his viewpoint on you without asking for yours in return. That being said, you may always be inventive in order to avoid engaging in talks that leave you feeling physically and mentally weary.

Everyone has strong feelings about some issues. Avoid the energy vampire's trigger themes if you wish to avoid negativity. For example, you may have a buddy who enjoys being negative about work. They can't stop complaining about how much they despise their jobs and how much their boss despises them. You feel worse for wear when you talk about work with your stated pal. When you discover that work is the triggering issue for this person, please stop talking about it. Choose themes about which they are less inclined to complain. You may guide the talks in your life in whatever manner you choose so that your conversation partner does not deplete you.

Finally, keep in mind that you do not have to cope with an energy vampire. It is well within your rights and freedom as a human being to refuse to engage with someone who is harmful to you. Never feel obligated to be patient with someone or to mend someone who is damaged. You're trying to live your best life and can't stretch yourself too thin by attempting to rescue everyone else. However sympathetic you are, it is crucial to acknowledge that some people's deep-seated troubles can only be treated with the assistance of a professional. It is OK to move away from someone who destroys your mojo. It is OK to inform a new boyfriend or girlfriend that you do not see the two of you working out. It is quite OK to choose self-preservation. You will never be able to save everyone.

CHAPTER 11

Type of Energy Vampire

Narcissist Vampires

A Narcissist Vampire is someone who constantly puts himself/herself in the spotlight. He/she always manages to bring every discussion back around to his/her favorite subject—him/herself. This is the sort of individual that will phone you and pretend to be interested in how you are. In less than a minute, the talk about you will be done. The rest of the talk will revolve around him/her.

Did you divorce your significant other? Prepare to hear about every narcissistic vampire breakup ever.

Has your eighth-grader been named to the honor roll? You'll learn how the offspring of a narcissist vampire is on the fast track to the Ivy League. Is his or her kid in kindergarten? This is irrelevant to the narcissistic vampire. It is always about him/her, and he/she must constantly be better. Vampire narcissists thrive at one-upmanship.

Victim Vampires

Victim vampires like being unhappy and spreading suffering. Have you had a horrible day? They had a bad day. The most annoying thing about victim vampires is that it is never their fault. The rest of the world has turned against them. They are victims of their surroundings. They always ask for help on how to solve their problems, but they rarely take it and often argue with you about why it won't work. Victim vampires will never run out of excuses.

Rage Vampires

Anger vampires, like victim vampires, believe that nothing is ever their fault. Unlike victim vampires, though, they go on the offense and blame others. A victim vampire will just complain about getting another flat tire and claim that this is evidence that the universe is working against him/her. An angry vampire will be accusatory and may allege anything absurd, such as that you realized his/her tire was low and didn't notify him/her because you are sabotaging his/her chances of receiving a promotion by making him/her/her late. Empaths are particularly uneasy around rage vampires. Empaths are affected by their feelings and energies, as well as their tendency to yell, rant, and get angry. This is a sensory overload for them.

Controlling Vampire

A dominating vampire will try to manipulate how you feel and what you do. If they don't like how you're feeling, they'll attempt to make you feel otherwise or just tell you how you feel. They will tell you what you need and desire while making you feel inferior. You are not an inferior human being. Controlling vampires are also extremely critical.

Drama Queen/King Vampire

The drama queen/king vampire must constantly be the focus of attention. They surely have pneumonia if they sneeze! They had a fantastic first date last night and are now almost engaged!

Drama queen/king vampires can transform practically any little situation into a major event. This is draining. Be cool; the calmer you are; the less energy they will have to feed on. Again, keep your limits in mind. Set boundaries in your personal life. Have a professional and impersonal demeanor with your coworkers. "I'm overjoyed that you found 'the one' and are already planning your wedding after only one date. But I'm afraid I must return to work. I've got a deadline!"

Monologue Vampires

Vampires with monologues never stop talking. Empaths are excellent listeners, and monologue vampires will drain you of all listening energy. They won't notice if you check your watch as a subtle signal that you need to end the discussion. They won't notice your crossed arms or efforts to enter the discussion. Since you don't have to engage in the discussion beyond a few nods and "mmm hmms," you'll have plenty of mental space to come up with a reason to terminate it.

Staking Your Energy Vampire

You are not required to maintain individuals in your life. If you have an energy vampire in your life, you should not retain him or her. They are harmful and will continue to depress you and drain your vitality. In folklore, venom from a bite may transmit vampirism. Similarly, the negativity transmitted by an energy vampire may be infectious. If you are constantly exposed to their negativity, they may succeed in turning you become a negative person like them. It would be a disgrace for you, your loved ones, and the world at large, given your empathic abilities. Don't let an energy vampire stop you from sharing great energy with the whole world.

The easiest technique to deal with an energy vampire is just to remove him or her from your life. Make a clean break and question yourself. In reality, removing someone from your life is not always feasible.

If a person V is merely a low-level energy vampire with redeeming traits, you may opt to retain him/her in your life. It is critical that you establish clear limits with this individual. You might also want to phase them out gradually so that you are not as involved in each other's life.

An energy vampire may be poisonous, but he or she is not always horrible. They might be a learned behavior from childhood or a protection mechanism. You might confront the individual about how they are making you feel. Individuals may be unaware that their actions are hurting until they decide to change! It is not advised to use the phrase "energy vampire" while discussing this issue. Adopt a more gentle approach. If the energy vampire is determined to make a positive change in his or her life, you may assist them in this endeavor. Therefore, proceed with care. The energy vampire may pretend to want to change but has no plans to do so. They can be trying to trick you into remaining in their lives and giving them even more attention and energy. Their path will be one of transition. You can help and support them, but don't let them use this as another chance to use your feelings and energy against you. You may have to let them go if you don't see them making good adjustments.

Dealing with Energy Vampires

Friends, family, coworkers, and peers are all energy vampires. You can't escape them entirely. Your paths will intersect at some time. You may be tempted to play the larger person as an empath eager to spread kindness with all and sundry. You can even search for a means to assist them in changing their behaviors. But keep in mind that these folks are energy and pleasure thieves. They will deflate you to the point that you will be unable to serve others, much alone yourself. They will squander your gift. It would be best if you approached them with care.

Some people choose to be vampires. Life has given them a bad hand. They are unhappy, and they do not like to see others happy. Instead of concentrating on themselves, they seek to make others unhappy so that they might be in the same boat. They are aware of what they are doing and are aware that they are causing harm to others. Yet they don't seem to mind.

These are some strategies for dealing with energy vampires:

Establish time limitations: If you must deal with them, create time constraints. If you allow them, these folks can keep you entertained for hours. Their terrible tales will dominate the talk the whole time. It's natural for everyone to have difficulties, but you can't have this one person always pretending to be in crisis. For example, you may state that you only have one hour to listen before having to attend to anything else. Maintain your time restriction; they will attempt to modify it as well.

Avoid disputing: debating with an energy vampire offers no results. They will come to you complaining about a broken relationship and constantly claiming to be innocent. You will attempt to persuade them of their role in the broken relationship. They will, as usual, deny any culpability. They will only insist on their innocence. Don't dispute; the discussion will continue until the kingdom arrives.

Be brief: Stick to short queries if you have to speak. Why? How? When? Such one-word questions will suffice.

Keep your views to yourself here. Voicing your beliefs just serves to perpetuate them, allowing others to dismiss them and establish their own as better.

Minimum response: An energy vampire attempts to elicit an emotional response from you. They tell you their tales of regret and ask you to feel sorry for them. When they say derogatory things, they want you to be angry and depressed. Please don›t give them the responses they›re expecting. Remain passive. With a straight face, listen. Make it clear that you are not affected by every whim. They win if your emotions shift as they engage you. Let them «win» at your cost. Nobody is worthy of it.

Avoid eye contact: Empaths are excellent listeners who like using all of their senses. This guideline does not apply if you are dealing with an energy vampire. Eye contact makes you more susceptible to what is stated, which is exactly what we want to avoid. Maintain little eye contact. Avoid sitting directly in front of the speaker. Simply give him/her a passing look. This may not seem to be very caring, but keep in mind that you are dealing with a strange man who is up to no good, and you must defend yourself.

Adhere to light topics: As previously said, Empaths thrive in meaningful interactions. Again, we must create an exception in this case. You don't want to get into a conversation about the meaning of life with an energy vampire. They'll do what they do best: water down your viewpoints, bring out their tragic experiences, and make the worst-case situation out of everything. Keep the discussion as light as possible. When they bring up their own difficulties, they just gloss over them without delving further. They are those that want to pull you through the muck as near to the surface as possible.

Minimize contact: Limit the number of times you have to interact with such folks. If they tend to drop by your house or business, inform them that they may only come with advance notice. What if they are truly from your home or office? These might be family members or coworkers, for example. Isn't this a little tricky? It would be best if you continued to decrease contact. If you have such a coworker, you are not required to share it with them. If you go out to lunch with a group, you may have a different coffee or bring a packed meal. At your workplace, avoid idle conversation. If you have such a person at home, spend more time in your room. It is not selfish to distance oneself from energy vampires; it is a question of self-preservation.

Be in a group: While you're alone, an energy vampire inflicts the most harm. Invite others to join the discussion. If a coworker picks you out to listen to your sorry tales, you might request that the others be included so that they can also have insight on the matter. Ask them to bring up the topic over lunch if they are hovering around your desk at work. You know the rest will be there, and you won't have to endure quite as much. Also, someone in the group may get the confidence to confront the energy vampire and call him or her out. Anticipate a disagreement, but the poisonous character may just reflect on it later and make some changes.

CHAPTER 12

What to Do When You Are the Vampire

You've probably already read this section and thought of times when you drained other people's energy. Maybe there are more than a few cases. Maybe you've discovered for the first time that you've been an energy vampire for as long as you can remember. You're undoubtedly feeling bad about all the energy you unintentionally drained from others. Maybe you're still in denial and think it's more like leaning on others and yelling than sucking their energy.

As you develop your self-awareness, you will begin to notice aspects of which you were previously unaware. You will see self-serving and damaging patterns of conduct. You will admit it to yourself when you have been unjust to others. You will see possibilities to be better than those you squandered. It'll be a real eye-opener for you. Recognizing whatever you discover without being too harsh on yourself would be best. We make mistakes because we are all flawed and not perfect. When you are oblivious to anything, you will make mistakes, behave selfishly, and harm others. Forgive yourself and know that you will no longer be able to use ignorance as an excuse for what you do in the future.

At the same time, recognize that other people do not exist to be used or to serve you. Some folks are dealing with issues that need assistance. Quit utilizing them more frequently than you help them. Consider how amazing the world would be if we paused to assist more frequently than we stopped to grumble or grieve. Everyone would be replenishing each other's energy reserves. We'd all have full tanks of good energy to get us where we needed to go. It seems very kumbaya when expressed in a way, but it is feasible. The world around you does not have to encompass the total population of your state. The world surrounding you may just be the loving ones with whom you share your home. Someone wise once stated that anybody who wants to change the world must first love their family. It doesn't go much deeper than that.

Make it a habit to pour yourself into the people you care about more than you receive from them. Be kind to your partner. Instead of grumbling about what occurred at work over lunch, consider a pleasant dinner date to make amends. Only you have control over the kind of energy you will have in your life. Go for the positive vibe. Make it clear to every bad energy that you have no space for it.

Tips to Help & Improve Yourself

If you believe you are an energy vampire, you are the only one who can assist and better yourself. Here are a few pointers that can help you improve:

1. The desire to alter oneself is the first and most important need. Let yourself have time to recuperate. This is a decision you must make for yourself. This entails accepting responsibility for your acts and changing your behavior.

2. List the habits that contribute to your becoming such a person. Acknowledge them and then make an effort to alter any such behavior in yourself. Do not humiliate yourself in the course of self-improvement.

3. Stop talking about yourself and start listening to others. This may be difficult for you, but if you want to alter yourself, you must listen to others.

4. Instead of blaming yourself, forgive yourself.

5. Know your limitations and never go beyond them.

Developing connections with others is vital, but avoid engaging with individuals who will put a strain on your mental health. As a result, pick your business properly and then cultivate a positive connection with those individuals.

Emotional Intelligence at Work

Emotions may arise as a consequence of how we perceive and respond to events, other people's actions, and other people's responses. We must exercise caution while dealing with emotions since they may alter how we react to a situation.

The capacity to identify, constructively express, and react to the emotions of others is referred to as emotional intelligence. In work, we form connections that are critical to our personal development and the company's success. A person with strong emotional intelligence might exhibit specific characteristics that boost their productivity, interpersonal interactions, and intrapersonal relationships.

Importance of Emotional Intelligence in the Workplace

Since they have self-awareness, empathy, and the ability to connect to others, people with high emotional intelligence may perform effectively in teams. On the other side, persons with low emotional intelligence prefer to work alone since they lack demonstrated potential or weakness. They lack empathy for others as well. As a result, while working in a group, disagreements might emerge.

Those who are emotionally savvy may create an atmosphere that encourages others to achieve. Employees will often labor for free if they are dissatisfied with their employment. They will always give their all in a work atmosphere that is kind, encouraging, and motivating and makes it easy to express themselves. To do this, you must follow a certain cycle while interacting with others.

- First, identify the emotion in the message.

- Second, be aware of your emotions and demonstrate empathy.

- Third, learn to recognize and manage your emotions.

- Lastly, practice self-regulation and empathy to regulate your emotions.

Emotional intelligence in the workplace is not merely a passing trend. Hiring an emotionally savvy team has real advantages.

1. Emotionally intelligent employees handle pressure better:

They see pressure as a challenge rather than a danger. Although others may be overwhelmed, they will remain cool and perform successfully. Whenever an issue arises, they may utilize it as a learning opportunity. They need less assistance from their supervisor to deal with stress.

2. Emotionally intelligent employees are better decision makers:

They are committed and aware of the dangers they are taking. They choose a mutually advantageous scenario and accept responsibility for their choice. We experience a lot of stress in our culture since our choices might affect our jobs and the firm's destiny. As a consequence, we often encounter disagreements and have difficulty engaging with others. This will not be a problem for emotionally savvy individuals since they manage emotional circumstances effectively. Since they can make judgments swiftly and effectively, this personnel are very successful in crucial circumstances.

3. Employees with high EQ handle conflicts better:

They can effectively listen to others. In every setting, they can sense how others are feeling. While they are present, they are not affected by other people's negative ideas. Disputes and conflicts seldom bother them, and they can solve problems gently and warmly.

4. High EQ employees are more motivated:

Emotions are a strong incentive to complete tasks. Those who are emotionally intelligent have a higher probability of inspiring colleagues to complete their tasks. Workers want to express themselves and get to know their managers. In exchange, these individuals will be very productive and offer exceptional outcomes.

5. Emotionally intelligent employees respond better to criticism:

They see criticism as a learning experience that can be used to better their career and interpersonal relationships. They recognize that the CEO simply wants the best for the firm, which gives them a feeling of fulfillment and responsibility. They will alter their conduct if they see their employer upset about anything they did. It is important to realize that not all criticism is bad. When it's constructive, the greatest thing you can do is utilize it as a learning opportunity.

How Do Hiring Managers Determine a Candidate's Emotional Intelligence?

Some claim that determining a candidate's emotional intelligence is difficult. Even if you wish to recruit people who have it, there are no easy solutions. Yet, there are certain methods to do this.

1. Presentation

The way a person displays themselves is quite important. Interviewers often pick applicants based on their presentation and overall demeanor. This shows how structured and goal-oriented the applicant is to the interviewer. They will also be able to assess the person's personality as well as what they enjoy and dislike. They will want to learn more about them if they like them.

2. Self-Interview

Emotionally intelligent individuals are not concerned with what others think of them but instead understand their strengths and flaws. Another characteristic of highly talented and emotionally intelligent persons is self-awareness.

3. Their Values and Beliefs

According to research, a person's value system is the most crucial factor in determining good emotional intelligence. Hiring managers feel that if a candidate's value system is not linked with the firm's values, a person's high emotional intelligence cannot be supported. Nevertheless, this is not the case. In reality, emotional intelligence helps people perform better for the firm, deliver better customer service, and pay more attention to their job. This is due to the caliber of their work and their desire to give back to society.

4. Their Emotional Content

Those who are emotionally savvy do not avoid situations or activities that make them feel vulnerable. Emotional content in the workplace is not uncommon. Emotionally aware individuals understand that work uncertainty, poor morale, low motivation, or low productivity are all caused by emotional content. Employees' emotional, mental, and physical wellness are all affected by emotional content. Because of this, emotional intelligence is also known as emotional management. You must have the great emotional intelligence to control your emotions.

5. The Relationship

Emotionally intelligent employees are also more loyal. They will prioritize the demands of the firm. This is due to their understanding that their duty is to work for the firm rather than for themselves. As a result, they might strengthen their connection with the employer. It is a more selfless connection since the employee devotes more of his or her time to what is best for the organization.

Employers search for emotional intelligence. It is critical to cultivating more of it on a daily basis. As a job seeker, you should know that employers prefer individuals who can work more efficiently and understand what is required of them. If the organization is seeking individuals with strong talents and high emotional intelligence, you could get the job and make the most of it. You do not need to see a psychologist to determine your emotional intelligence. You may learn it for yourself by using the information given here. You may also be aware of how to work with or develop your emotional intelligence.

Here are seven techniques to exhibit your emotional intelligence at a job interview.

Listen Actively

Individuals often fail because they place too much emphasis on the reaction rather than the message. Listen attentively before answering any inquiry. Interviewers prefer thorough replies to inquiries over hasty, unprepared ones. If you're not sure about a question, ask the interviewer.

Express Your Emotions According to Your Needs

You may need to express what you observe in your replies at times. Interviewees may express emotions that may not correspond to their statements, such as terror. Creating a relationship with your interviewer will be easier if you show the appropriate emotion. When required, real excitement is acceptable but not excessive.

Give Credit Where Credit Is Due

Don't attempt to bluff, even if your success was the product of teamwork with other stakeholders. Instead, give credit where it is due. When possible, acknowledge the partner for their contribution to your achievement, whether through project work or otherwise.

Show Your Interest in Growing More

Don't be arrogant about the information you've gained. Do not exhibit a lack of desire to learn more and take on new tasks. It is critical to highlight how you intend to overcome your deficiencies while articulating them. You might also emphasize your strengths and why you perceive yourself as strong.

Boldly Express Any Point of Contradiction.

You should not accept all inputs automatically but rather express your opinions if the interviewer makes a contradicting assertion. Nonetheless, do so calmly and precisely. Additionally, inform the interviewer how you intend to adjust to your new surroundings.

Learn From Your Mistakes

When things go off the rails, an interviewer may ask you certain questions. You do not have to assume responsibility for other people's errors; instead, accept responsibility and learn from any mistakes that may arise. But, before answering such questions, it is necessary to think critically and pick the most appropriate emotions.

Ask Questions

The interviewer may enable you to ask questions at the conclusion of the session. Demonstrate emotion in response to various information stated by the interviewer. You may also express your interest in learning more about the firm.

CHAPTER 14

Emotional Intelligence at Home

Individuals who lack emotional intelligence make horrible partners in relationships. While it is not the be-all and end-all of a relationship, emotional intelligence is a significant factor. You would be better off not being close to someone who isn't emotionally mature because they will always fall short of your expectations, at least when it comes to feelings.

Dating someone who has a poor EQ may be quite difficult. It might prevent you from experiencing all of the perks and conveniences that come with being in a relationship. A spouse with a poor EQ may also be detrimental to your self-esteem. Regrettably, many individuals are unaware of how to determine if their spouse or another loved one has a low EQ. You may have heard a friend say that her partner is never sensitive to her emotions or that he often screams when they argue. Although you may have recognized that this is incorrect, you were most likely unaware of the link between such conduct and poor emotional intelligence.

Emotions may accelerate relationships. It is critical to regulating such emotions to maintain effective communication within a partnership or marriage. When partners work together to improve their emotional intelligence, it's easy to get past disagreements, find common ground, and grow closer. Knowing the power of emotions to impact our conduct and affect others (both positively and adversely) and learning how to manage them, particularly when we are under stress.

People base their choices on their emotions and sentiments. If you can detect your emotions, you can improve your relationships with others.

Couples may develop emotional intelligence by using these five suggestions. The five suggestions below will help couples develop emotional intelligence.

1. Validating Feelings

It is useful for confirming another person's sentiments. When people feel appreciated, they are more willing to talk freely. Emotions should be validated. Don't bother looking at the sides. Respond to what your husband stated instead. This might be represented by a woman complaining that you don't remove your clothing from the living room. You may relieve your frustration by simply picking up your garments. You may support your wife's emotion by saying something like, "Do you feel anxious when my clothes aren't picked up?"

2. Clarifying the Way to Understand

It is important to confirm what people are feeling and saying to avoid misunderstandings that could lead to arguments.

To demonstrate that you are listening, use active listening skills and repeat what your companion stated. Let's take tip number one as an example and explain it. Did I get it right? "You become agitated when you don't pick up my clothing. If you did, you'd be less frustrated."

3. Finding Solutions

You should be part of the solution, not the cause. Your companion may require assistance with something. You might engage your wife in the solution by putting a hamper in your wardrobe and asking him to put his clothing inside.

4. Being Optimistic

Stress management becomes simpler when you focus on the good aspects of life. Optimism has been shown in studies to improve overall health.

There are several things you may do to improve your mood. Every day, you may tell your partner how much you adore them.

5. Accepting the Best of Others

You may be able to put your confidence in your spouse's good intentions, and they may just meet your expectations. If you assume the best, you will feel better. Negative thoughts may bring you down. You may practice getting the most out of your partner by identifying and sharing a good feature in your relationship.

Dealing With a Partner Who Has Low Emotional Intelligence

What do you do if your partner's lack of emotional intelligence is driving you crazy? Should you throw them out or give them a chance to improve? Logistically, eliminating those with poor emotional intelligence is easy. We all know, however, that the heart wants what the heart desires. Moreover, if you removed all of the individuals with low EQ from your life, you'd probably be left with just one or two people. Yeah, having a high EQ is uncommon. This takes us to the advice for dealing with someone you love but who sometimes makes you want to claw your eyes out.

Tip #1: Address the elephant in the room early on.

When two lovebirds first meet, they want the other to believe they are perfect little angels who can do no wrong. They go on dates, make each other laugh, and only say nice things to each other. When one of them makes a mistake, such as snapping at a poor waiter who is merely trying to do his job, the other enamored lovebird ignores it and chalks it up to a difficult day. The lovebird is prepared to forgive and forget, even if it happens again at another restaurant. That is until it happens within the safe confines of their loving home. The lovebird then recognizes that one individual can't experience seven unpleasant days in a row unless they are the source of the awful days.

You are the lovebird in the story, and the lesson is that you should say something when you see bad behavior, especially if it happens more than once. Yes, your boyfriend is permitted to have one gloomy day when he refuses to speak to anybody, but five days is pushing it. How can you have a relationship with someone who is unable to express their emotions? Bring it up if anything annoys you about your spouse (particularly if it implies poor EQ). Don't let it fester and consume you with bitterness. Couples who talk freely in a relationship have a greater probability of being together for longer.

Tip #2: Watch your tone

So you've taken a few emotional intelligence tests (including the one in Chapter 8 of this book) and determined that you clearly outperform your spouse in terms of emotional intelligence. What comes next? Do you rule over them? Do you treat them as if they are a little person because they struggle with their emotions? Certainly not. Because doing so implies that the tests were erroneous, therapists have often said that how a couple communicates with each other significantly impacts how long they remain together.

Some individuals have low EQ not because they want to but because they don't know any different. As an emotionally intelligent partner or spouse, your responsibility is to bring your partner around. The side on which individuals converse with empathy and respect. The side of individuals who are excellent listeners and do not interrupt others while they are speaking. If you talk down to your spouse about how much smarter you are emotionally, he or she will start to dislike you. Note that your spouse is probably unaware of their lack of emotional intelligence (see the section on self-awareness in Chapter

2 for more on this). Don't make things more difficult for them by condescending to them.

Tip #3: Be realistic about your expectations

You've always suspected that your spouse has a low EQ, and this book has confirmed your suspicions by presenting solid proof of what EQ is and is not. What happens next? Should you give this book to your spouse and insist that they read it from beginning to end and report back to you in a week with a better EQ? Certainly not. That is not the case.

Certainly, some components of emotional intelligence may be practiced and mastered in a matter of days. You may, for example, strive to be a good listener by always allowing the other person to complete speaking before responding. This is a strategy that can be put into action in a couple of days. But, learning to be in touch with emotions, to be a better communicator, and to care for others may take a little longer. Your companion may not even be interested. When you propose that they do this or that, they may object. Remember that people with low EQ dislike change. Converting your lover will not be an easy task. Yet, suppose your spouse genuinely loves you and is devoted to your relationship. In that case, you may assist them in taking the small steps necessary for the relationship to become even more satisfying than it now is.

Tip #4: Remember it's okay to fight

Every partnership has its own set of issues. A relationship can never be without disagreements unless both partners are hesitant to express their actual feelings. Fights help to develop bonds. They provide a forum for couples to express sentiments that have been concealed deep inside. Please do not feel guilty or ashamed about your disagreements, whether they be about EQ or anything else. Even the most emotionally sophisticated individuals struggle with their loved ones. They just know better than to shout, curse, or strike. You're on the correct road as long as you're battling without tearing each other down.

Tip #5: Let the other person choose to change

You may, in fact, encourage another individual to change by modeling the right conduct. You can never compel someone who does not want to change to change. Change is a personal choice that an individual must make when they are ready. If your spouse acts in a way that you find emotionally immature, they must come to terms with the fact that they are wrong and then resolve to change. This may take a long time and may even seem impossible at first. Waiting for them to be ready may need all of your patience. Only you will be able to determine if they are worth the wait.

Tip #6: Sometimes you'll have to walk away

Suppose you've been working with a partner who clearly has a poor EQ for a long period of time. This spouse does not understand your sentiments; they openly insult you, have no qualms about shouting, are usually theatrical about something, and cannot see the issue. When you attempt to discuss these difficulties with your spouse, you are treated with frigid treatment. What are you going to do?

You have to cut the cord on a failing relationship at some time. Relationships are not recyclable polymers that you can save and reuse after you've finished using them for their intended purpose. A relationship is meant to be a good thing in your life. If your spouse shows evidence of poor or nonexistent emotional intelligence, such as being emotionally abusive, you have every right to leave. In fact, you should not only stroll but also sprint as rapidly as your high EQ heels will allow. Someone out there who is self-aware and driven is certain to value a respectful relationship with an emotionally mature adult like yourself.

CHAPTER 15

Busting the Myths About Emotional Intelligence

There are some common misunderstandings about emotional intelligence and many other subjects. Throughout this book, you've probably been able to see where you've been wrong about emotional intelligence and how things really are. This chapter is all about clearing up the many false beliefs that people have about EQ. Some of the myths are amusing, while others are ludicrous. Since that EQ is concerned with emotion, it is not surprising that different emotions are exhibited on the same topic. Dig in to discover what is true and what isn't regarding emotional intelligence.

Myth: Emotional intelligence is a woman's area

Truth: Emotional intelligence is a skill that applies to both men and women.

For the longest time, numerous outlets have fostered the idea that women are more emotional than men. As a result, most people primarily think of women when they hear the term "emotional intelligence." Nothing could be farther from the truth. First and foremost, the assumption that women are the more emotional members of the human species is not substantiated by biology. As scientists looked into these things, they found that the people they talked to were more likely to act in a way that was expected by their cultures than in a way that was in line with nature. In other words, women may act more emotionally because society or culture expects it of them, but men may suppress their emotions for the same reason.

We can all feel emotions, no matter what gender we are, so we need to know how to understand and control them. Even if a parallel world existed in which guys were practically incapable of feeling emotions, they would still have to deal with women who plainly do. As a result, emotional intelligence is a scale that these parallel universe guys would need to engage with parallel universe females.

Myth: Emotional intelligence is the sole determinant for success in life.

Truth: Many factors determine whether you will be successful in life and EQ happens to be one of them.

Emotional intelligence may help you in many ways. When you can read and connect to people well, you do not face as many challenges as someone with a poor EQ. Yet, EQ is not a one-stop shop for success. Success requires a mix of intelligence, hard effort, opportunity or chance, and, at times, pure luck. Being low on EQ does not inherently predispose you to failure. In reality, there are several occupations where individuals may achieve great success only by using their intelligence.

For an engineer, for example, it may be necessary to have an extremely high IQ in order to absorb topics effortlessly. The same engineer might have a low EQ and yet be extremely successful since their job requires brains above emotional intelligence. The engineer may struggle with personal connections and will most likely never assume a managerial role, but they will be successful in their own way.

Myth: Emotional intelligence is about being nice.

Truth: Emotional intelligence is more than just being nice.

Over the years, Nice has been linked with being a pushover or a doormat. When individuals hear that someone is good, they begin to fantasize about how they may humiliate that person. Emotional intelligence is about being kind if you define pleasantness as the ability to accept other people's personalities and quirks. Nevertheless, if your idea of this kind is someone who says yes to every request and does not have their own voice, you are far from understanding emotional intelligence. You are not a yes-man by virtue of your emotional intelligence. In reality, emotional intelligence provides you with all of the abilities you need to say no as often as you need to, without apology.

Myth: You're either born with emotional intelligence or not.

Truth: You can learn to become more emotionally intelligent.

Emotional intelligence is not the same as height, in which you are born either tall or short and are condemned never to reach the upper shelves or to be the brunt of height jokes. Indeed, some individuals are more adept at understanding emotional intelligence than others. This may be determined by how people are born and reared, their experiences, and a variety of other things with which they interact as adults. Most individuals, on the other hand, are emotionally intelligent. Even psychopaths, who are unable to experience emotions like the rest of us, may imitate emotional intelligence. You are emotionally intelligent if you are a fully functioning human being with a broad spectrum of emotions.

Myth: Everyone that knows how to charm people is emotionally intelligent.

Truth: Sometimes there is more than emotional intelligence behind the charm.

Some of the loveliest individuals you know are also some of the most dangerous people you'll ever meet. Just because someone understands when and how to grin in your face does not imply they have a high EQ. They might just be manipulative. Psychopaths, for example, know how to blend in and play the character of Mr. Sociable Man to perfection. Although an emotionally competent person may make you feel calm and comfortable without violating your personal space, a psychopath attempting to gain your trust may be more pushy, insistent, and full-on in an uncomfortable way. Trusting your gut instinct, monitoring if someone's behaviors match their statements, and noting how you feel after each conversation are all tricks you may use to assess whether you're dealing with high EQ or psychopathy. If you leave talks feeling exhausted and uncertain, you may be dealing with an energy vampire rather than an emotionally savvy individual.

Myth: Introverts are not usually emotionally intelligent.

Truth: Introverts can be as emotionally intelligent as anyone else.

People often think of introverts as shy and socially awkward, with little to no chance of ever being good at regular social interactions. Although this may be true in certain cases, it is not the academic definition of an introvert. An introvert is just someone who likes to go inside themselves for stimulation rather than seeking it from their surroundings. An introvert is happy in their own company and would rather be quiet than speak. The extrovert lacks emotional intelligence and is an introvert's worst nightmare. Nevertheless, just because someone likes to be quiet does not always indicate that they lack emotional intelligence. In fact, the fact that introverts are inward-looking indicates that they have worked out the self-awareness aspect of EQ. Nevertheless, since introverts are so immersed in their worlds (in the most selfless manner imaginable), they must work a bit more to bring themselves out into their exterior surroundings.

Given that introversion is a personality type and that personalities are not considered to be dynamic, an introvert will often confront the difficult challenge of opening up their world to other people. For example, you cannot be sympathetic to the pain of others unless you are aware of their pain. To become aware of this pain, you must first communicate with this individual so that they may confirm that they are truly having a poor day. An introvert may find this nearly too much to ask.

The good news is that emotional intelligence is a talent that can be mastered. Introverts, like people with other types of personalities, may notice the signs they need to learn in order to understand how people feel. In truth, some introverts are quite emotionally sophisticated. When they are in a group, they know how to carry themselves. They recognize that some situations need them to leave the safety of their shells. When they return home, they silently retire to the protection of their shell until new circumstances force them to emerge.

Myth: Emotional intelligence is only important for people in leadership roles or in particular professions.

Truth: Emotional intelligence makes your life easier regardless of who you are.

When you are in a leadership position, your lack of emotional intelligence will be more noticeable and destructive than a lack of emotional intelligence in the individuals you lead or in any other person. When it comes to emotional intelligence, the saying "with great power comes tremendous responsibility" could not be more accurate. When you are a leader or boss, your every action is scrutinized. People will notice how you interact with your subordinates, show care and regard for others, handle difficult circumstances, and even manage yourself. Your teams will also turn to you to demonstrate the kind of conduct they should mimic and to be their business and interpersonal mentors. Consider yourself in this situation if you don't have emotional intelligence. More than likely, you will be completely overwhelmed.

Having said that, emotional intelligence is a skill that everyone should possess. You do not need to be anybody's boss to appreciate the benefits that come with being self-aware and self-regulating. How about motivation? Everyone may benefit from a little more intrinsic motivation and enthusiasm in their life. Motivation is what provides the fuel to get you all you need in life. If nothing else, strive to be emotionally knowledgeable in order to have better personal interactions in your life. We may all benefit from some of those.

CHAPTER 16

Are You Emotionally Intelligent?

Test DISC, Test EQ

This quiz is meant to help you figure out what your strengths and weaknesses are when it comes to emotional intelligence. If the results show that you are emotionally smart, you can keep doing what you've been doing. If you discover at the conclusion of the test that you have not been acting in an emotionally intelligent way, this should not make you feel awful. This should instead act as an incentive for you to accomplish more and be better.

You may begin this exam whenever you are ready. If it isn't right now, you may stop reading, come back later, or move straight to the end. Proceed if you are ready to take the quiz right now. The test's rules are straightforward. Just respond yes or no to the questions below, and your score will be calculated at the end. Remember to be honest in your responses. If you want to gain an accurate picture of your emotional intelligence, you must remain impartial and honest.

Emotional Intelligence Quiz

Most of the time, you can define your feelings and name them using a large vocabulary. You don't simply declare whether you're OK or not. Instead, you'll be able to tell when you're annoyed, unhappy, angry, stressed out, sad, etc. TRUE/FALSE

You've never considered yourself so self-absorbed, selfish, or self-serving that you don't care what's happening around you. You have a natural desire to learn more about the people around you. Even though you are introverted, you like observing and learning more about the individuals you encounter in your daily life. TRUE/FALSE

You are adaptable to change. You have a flexible mindset and feel that change is as beneficial as rest. You believe that one of the most interesting aspects of life is change. TRUE/FALSE

You are well aware of your strengths and can describe your weaknesses. You're aware of the folks you get along with and those that irritate you. TRUE/FALSE

Humans are not easily duped. You can quickly discern their character, even if they attempt to pass themselves off as someone else. When it comes to humans, very few things surprise you. TRUE/FALSE

You pride yourself on having thick skin. You don't go about hunting for reasons to be outraged. You like self-deprecating humor and don't mind being the punchline of a joke until it crosses appropriate lines. TRUE/FALSE

You learn from your errors instead of dwelling on them. You are aware that it is natural for humans to make errors from time to time. Failure is seen as a learning opportunity rather than a reflection of your self-worth. TRUE/FALSE

You may forgive people who have harmed you because you know what is best for yourself. Grudges have no place in your life, and you recover fast from the misdeeds of others. TRUE/FALSE

When you have contact with a toxic person, you know how to manage them in a manner that does not emotionally exhaust you. You make every effort, however difficult, to see things from the poisonous person's point of view. You understand how to safeguard your energy while dealing with poisonous people. TRUE/FALSE

You don't strive for perfection because you recognize that it is just an idea that exists in people's imaginations and not in reality. You do not expect perfection from yourself, your loved ones, or even the people you work with. You just want to be able to claim that you did your best under the circumstances. TRUE/FALSE

You know when you need to get away from the strains of regular life, and you do so without hesitation. You've never felt obligated to be accessible to everyone and everything all the time. You can simply switch off and decompress because you understand how vital it is for your physical, mental, and emotional health. TRUE/ FALSE

You are picky about what you put into your body. You understand that what you eat greatly impacts how you feel, and you know better than to let dangerous substances into your system. You keep an eye on what you eat without becoming obsessed with it. TRUE/FALSE.

Sleep is a top priority for you. You don't stay up all night doing things that can be done later. You understand how essential sleep is in your life since it helps your brain to recover and replenish. You have a habit of sleeping at the same hour every night. TRUE/FALSE.

You are nice to yourself. Self-doubt has no place in your life. You don't let yourself be harsh or judgmental of yourself. Instead of beating yourself up for every shortcoming, you forgive yourself for your failures and search for methods to better yourself. TRUE/FALSE

You are self-assured and do not need confirmation from others. You are proud of your successes and know how to enjoy both major and minor victories. Don't worry about what other people think of you since what counts is what you think about yourself. You don't let somebody into your life which takes away your pleasure. TRUE/FALSE

How many questions did you correctly answer? Based on your responses, the table below displays your emotional intelligence score.

Emotional Intelligence Rating

15: Very High EQ

You are in touch with your emotions, have a strong sense of your own identity, and are driven to be true to yourself. You appreciate other people's emotions without allowing them to control your life. You're probably entertaining to be around since you're emotionally mature and can take a joke or two. Your coworkers and friends like you more than you realize. Not that it matters to you in any case.

10-14: High EQ

You know who you are and how to read people. You are sympathetic to others but do not allow them to drain your energy. You understand the value of emotional intelligence and will always bite your tongue before lashing out at anybody. You like yourself and can describe your objectives, aspirations, and accomplishments. You have ideas, but you also tolerate opposing viewpoints without becoming agitated.

5-9: Average EQ

You get along with most people and like yourself most of the time. Nonetheless, you continue to deal with many issues with yourself, your emotions, and other people. You have good days when you seem to do and say the right things and terrible days when your foot is always in your mouth. You might be too harsh on yourself at times, and there are times when you wish you could go back in time and rectify your errors. You take too long to forgive yourself and others and still harbor grudges against certain people. You want you could be a better person, but you don't know how (hopefully, this book has solved that question).

0-4: Low EQ

If your life narrative were produced into a TV show, it would be a lousy comedy that would be terminated after one season. You don't know who you are and seem to upset everyone everywhere you go. You continuously feel bad about yourself and your life. Every morning, you fight to get out of bed. Your coworkers don't appear to like you, and your supervisor is undoubtedly thinking of terminating you. You have difficulty dating, and if you are in a relationship or married, you can't seem to get your spouse to quit bickering with you. You shout when you're furious, and you've even thrown a few things in your rage. The emotions in your life manifest in severe ways. You are never just content or calm. You are more likely to be highly angry/agitated/frustrated than moderately angry/agitated/frustrated. There are possibilities and hope for you to become more emotionally sophisticated, but you must work really hard to fix all of your current concerns.

CHAPTER 17

Putting It into Practice

Now that you know what you can do to improve your EQ, it's important to establish a strategy for yourself so that you can start benefiting yourself and reaching your objectives. Please keep in mind that change may be difficult, particularly when you are learning new abilities and conditioning your body and mind to behave differently. It's time to put all you've learned into action and start seeing results!

It is often said that it takes 21 days to become a habit. With this in mind, it will take many weeks for each skill to become ingrained in your mind and body, and that is only if you practice them every day. Thankfully, you can practice many talents at once. Every day, you will have several chances to use your new emotional intelligence skills, and many of these situations will enable you to practice more than one ability at once. Some are more situational, and you may have to wait even longer before you can work on them. For example, how often you show cultural and social awareness will depend on how often you are exposed to different cultures.

If you feel overwhelmed or believe it is impossible, make a step-by-step strategy for yourself. Rather than focusing on the big picture, consider creating smaller objectives for yourself. The most effective technique to create a goal is to put out your overall aim, such as "raising your chances of success." Next, put out three measures to achieve that objective, such as "increasing EQ," "getting a better career," or "establishing a long-term loving connection." After you've put out your three stages, divide them into three smaller steps.

You'll have nine minor tasks to complete before completing the three phases that will bring you to your final objective. It may seem that you have more to accomplish, but focusing on one or two of the simplest actions at a time will allow you to do them much more quickly. A little step requires less time, energy, and concentration than a large objective. Hence, divide your objectives into smaller segments and create a self-help strategy that is tailored to your specific needs.

After determining your starting point, choose three of the abilities and methodologies given in that chapter to focus on first. Make a strategy for strengthening these talents and integrating them into your everyday life. If they are based on events, make a list of events that will take place in the following three weeks and plan out how you will use your newly acquired talents. When it comes down to it, these abilities are similar to muscles. It would help if you continued to exercise them in order for them to stay robust.

It is a good idea to choose three abilities that do not have many overlaps and cannot be employed in the same scenarios. This allows you to practice strategies that will benefit you in a variety of situations. If you believe you have a decent grasp on those three talents and believe the idea of emotional intelligence requires more effort, choose another three and begin working on them. You may work on all of the abilities supplied in each chapter segment, or you can pick and select the ones that will be most valuable to you and your success.

After completing your first three, if you believe you have a decent grasp on that subject, go on to the next one and choose three new talents to concentrate on. Practice as many skills and procedures as you need to feel confident in that area before moving on to the next. Now, if you finish one component and discover you didn't go as far as you desired, just go back and take up another three things from your prior notion of study. Please don't consider this a failure; it isn't. Consider it a rest stop.

Keep in mind that your body and brain are being physically reprogrammed and rewired to respond and behave differently. It may sometimes revert to its old programming. That is just a system problem that may be resolved by brushing up on the new code. Don't get disappointed if you believe you already have a high level of self-awareness and go straight into self-management, only to discover you don't have as much as you thought. This whole procedure is a great self-discovery and self-improvement exercise. You're going to discover a lot about yourself, and isn't that the point? Thus, if you discover something unexpected, make it work for you. Use it as proof that your self-discovery is effective!

Relationship management is focused on last since it is the culmination of all the skills and approaches learned up to that time. It's a fantastic place to conclude since it ties everything together and even asks you to build on those ideas for more sophisticated applications. Suppose relationship management is your sole goal or the only area in which you need to improve. In that case, you may find it useful to review the list of skills and topics for self-awareness, self-management, and social awareness to see if there are any skills you need to brush up on before diving into relationship management.

It is really beneficial to keep an emotional diary throughout this period. Maintaining a record of what works and what doesn't. This notebook will be a valuable tool for self-reflection and evaluating your own development and triumphs and may serve as a personal textbook or guide for achieving your own success. When focusing on developing your EQ, don't be shocked if your overall objectives, aspirations, or wants shift as a result of your own development. This often occurs since personal development and change affect all parts of your existence. Who you were before you began this trip had different desires than the person you became as a result of the adventure. Keep your objectives and ambitions up to date as you grow.

Your strategy for increasing your EQ will be heavily influenced by your own lifestyle and what you want to achieve from this approach. Not everyone will have the same objectives or areas to develop on. That is why Chapters 4 and 5 provide so many tools and abilities to employ. Make your strategy based on what you know you need to work on initially. Throughout the process, you may discover additional areas that may benefit from modification. On the other hand, you may realize that you are much better off in several areas than you previously assumed. Make a point of celebrating all of your tiny successes and major achievements. This will keep you inspired to continue.

Conclusion

In spite of what you might think when you hear the term "emotional intelligence," it's not just about knowing your own feelings. That is just one aspect of it. Understanding other people's emotions is a key component of emotional intelligence, which has both personal and professional advantages. We may not always be able to control others' emotions, but we can always control our own. Emotional intelligence is being able to control how you treat people, respond appropriately to how they feel, and not let your own feelings get in the way of your ability to do things well. It's also about knowing when to take charge, pull aside, and allow people to work through problems independently.

Emotional intelligence was first thought of in the late 20th century when it became clear that IQ wasn't the best way to predict how successful someone would be in life. Certain IQ tests have been demonstrated to be virtually uniformly faulty. It was proposed that a person's total level of EQ may be a far more reliable predictor of overall success in life.

Self-awareness and self-regulation are the two most important parts of emotional intelligence. They both have to do with being able to recognize one's own feelings and change them in a way that fits the current situation. To develop emotional intelligence, people must be able to recognize their own feelings and know when they are appropriate or not. Individuals with greater emotional intelligence are less stressed, more proactive in their emotions, and have superior social skills. Reduced melancholy, anxiety, and stress are also associated with emotional intelligence. The more work you put into developing your emotional intelligence, the more advantageous it will be for you and the people around you. Self-awareness is the ability to understand your own feelings and how they affect your body and mind. Each individual will perceive their emotions differently. It would help if you also understood that there is no universally correct or incorrect way to experience anything. A person's circumstances might also influence how they feel. For instance, a student might be nervous before a long test, but if they do well on that day, they will be happy and relieved. From one minute to the next, emotions might fluctuate dramatically. This notion is known as "emotional whiplash." You might be angry about something, but if someone does something nice for you, you might feel thankful right away.

Self-awareness also assists individuals in recognizing when their emotions are interfering with their interactions with others. It is important to be aware of your emotions and how they impact others around you since too much negativity may harm relationships and make it difficult to connect with people. People who have trouble naming their feelings may think that the problem is always the fault of someone else.

"It's all right to be passionate. It's all right to have strong feelings. However, what you do with those feelings matters most." Sir John Lennon.